Indus Journey

IMRAN KHAN

Indus Journey

A personal view of
PAKISTAN

Photographs by Mike Goldwater

Chatto & Windus
LONDON

Published in 1990 by
Chatto & Windus Limited
20 Vauxhall Bridge Road
London SW1V 2SA

A CIP catalogue record for this book is available
from the British Library.

ISBN 0 7011 3527 1

Text copyright © Imran Khan 1990
Photographs copyright © Mike Goldwater 1990
Imran Khan has asserted his right to be
identified as the author of this work.

Phototypeset by Rowland Phototypesetting Limited
Bury St Edmunds, Suffolk
Printed in Great Britain by
Butler & Tanner Limited, Frome, Somerset

To the
dwindling forests and wildlife
of Pakistan

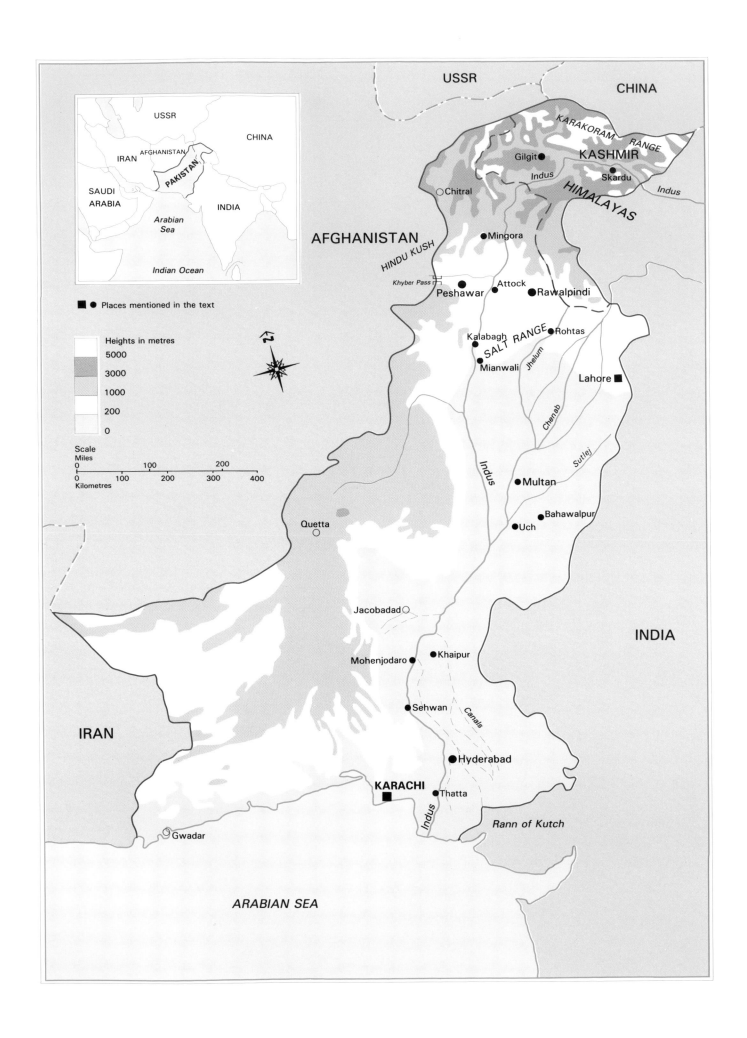

USSR

CHINA

KASHMIR

KARAKORAM RANGE

Gilgit ●

● Skardu

Indus

Indus

○ Chitral

HIMALAYAS

AFGHANISTAN

HINDU KUSH

● Mingora

Khyber Pass ⊞

Peshawar ●   ● Attock   ● Rawalpindi

Kalabagh ●   *SALT RANGE* ● Rohtas

● Mianwali   *Jhelum*

Lahore ■

Chenab

Sutlej

● Multan

Quetta ○

Indus

● Bahawalpur

● Uch

INDIA

Jacobadad ○

● Khaipur

Mohenjodaro ●

● Sehwan

Canals

IRAN

● Hyderabad

KARACHI
■   ● Thatta

Rann of Kutch

○ Gwadar

ARABIAN SEA

USSR

IRAN   AFGHANISTAN   CHINA

PAKISTAN

SAUDI
ARABIA   INDIA

*Arabian
Sea*

Indian Ocean

■ ● Places mentioned in the text

Heights in metres

5000
3000
1000
200
0

Scale
Miles
0   100   200
0   100   200   300   400
Kilometres

Contents

Introduction

I first thought of writing a book about the Indus
– and what it has meant to me, and to my
country – when friends from abroad used to
complain that there was very little to read about
Pakistan. A great deal had been written about
India, which had not only given its name to the
entire sub-continent but had, until Partition,
included what is now Pakistan; but Pakistan
itself, so much younger a country, had been
relatively neglected. Not only did foreign visitors have no real idea of what to expect – and
were often amazed at the sheer variety of the

country – but Pakistanis themselves, and particularly those living in the cities, were equally ill-informed. I decided that I would write a book about the Indus river, which runs the entire length of the country (and, incidentally, gave the sub-continent and our neighbour to the east their names through its Sanskrit name of 'Sindhu') so as to introduce visitors and my fellow-countrymen to the ways in which the country changes from north to south, from the arid deserts of Sindh to the Himalayas, and from the North-West Frontier to the Punjab, where I grew up and went to school. My own life, like that of Pakistan itself, has been inextricably interwoven with the Indus and its tributaries, and I hope that my book will shed light on my country and its people.

One of the great rivers of the world, with an annual flow twice that of the Nile and three times that of the Tigris and Euphrates combined, the Indus rises in the high, windswept mountains of Tibet, and empties into the Arabian Sea some 1800 miles later. From Tibet it flows in a north-westerly direction, between the Himalayas and the Karakoram, through the Indian territory of Ladakh before entering Pakistan in Baltistan in the remote Northern Areas; and from there on it remains an exclusively Pakistani river. Pakistan contains many of the world's highest mountains, and the Indus begins its life in what is known as the roof of the world, picking its way between permanently snow-capped mountains, fed by glaciers, and running through vertical, sunless gorges thousands of feet deep. The inhabitants of Baltistan call it the 'lion river', and it is almost impossible to associate this rapidly flowing torrent with the placid, shallow, slow-moving river that meanders through the plains of the Lower Punjab and Sindh, over ten miles wide in places, with buffalo splashing in the shallows and palm trees growing along its banks. Near Gilgit, in the mountainous far north,

PREVIOUS PAGES: LEFT *The Indus at Hund, where Alexander the Great made his famous crossing into north-west India.*
ABOVE *Hand-made sandals from my father's village.*

the Indus suddenly changes direction, and begins the long journey south, towards the sea. For hundreds of miles yet the mountains hem it in – the Himalayas on the left bank, the Hindu Kush on the right – and it remains narrow and fast-flowing, more often than not racing through gorges, until it reaches the town of Kalabagh, on the very edge of the Salt Range. At Kalabagh the Indus debouches – very suddenly – onto the plain; within a hundred yards of the bridge there it is a mile wide, and a mile further on it is ten miles wide; and from here, 700 feet above sea level, to the delta, 950 miles to the south, it becomes a very different kind of river, with a gradient of less than nine inches to the mile.

Such, then, is the course of the Indus: but I decided that I would make the journey in reverse, starting at Thatta near the delta and

Breakfast on the Indus with my cousin, Hameed Niazi.
OVERLEAF *Sunset on the lower reaches of the Indus.*

3

ending in Skardu in the Himalayas, describing various places along the river and its tributaries that I found particularly fascinating or that meant a great deal to me, and so evoking the changing life and culture of Pakistan itself, from the Baluchis of Sindh and my own people, the Pathans, to the mysterious, Dravidian dwellers by Lake Manchnar and the Tibetan-like inhabitants of Baltistan.

Like all great rivers, the Indus has been both a barrier and a focus of attraction to settlers and invaders. Only in the past forty years or so have we become fully aware of the great pre-Aryan civilisation that flourished in the Indus Valley some 2500 years BC, the equal and the contemporary of those of ancient Egypt and Mesopotamia, the remains of which can be found at Mohenjodaro★ in Sindh, and Harappa in the Punjab. This highly sophisticated culture, which lasted for over a thousand years, vanished as mysteriously as it had arrived; whether it was destroyed by Aryan armies is a matter of debate, but the arrival of the Aryans – nomadic peoples from Central Asia, pouring over what became known much later as the North-West Frontier to plunder and eventually settle the fertile, placid lands of the Indus Valley – set a pattern that was to be repeated over the next three thousand years by the Huns, the Scythians, the Pathans, the Turkomen and the Mongols. Not surprising, perhaps, the Indus and the territories to either side of it have been absorbed and regurgitated by empire after empire. Darius I of Persia conquered the Indus Valley, which then formed the frontier between Persia itself and India proper, and became (between the Salt Range and the Arabian Sea) the twentieth satrapy of his empire. More famously, Alexander the Great crossed the Hindu Kush after garrisoning Kabul and, a year later, ferried his army across the Indus at Hund, before making his way, with 2000 ships, down the Jhelum and the Indus to the delta, and so eventually – though Alexander himself died en route – back to Greece. Islam penetrated India up the Indus Valley, initially by means of the Arab invasions of 711 AD

*People resting in the Shah Jehan Mosque. Even at the
hottest time of the day it remains cool inside the mosque.*

★ The modern-day spelling in Pakistan is Moenjodaro; we have adopted the original phonetic transliteration throughout this book.

by the seventeen-year-old Muhammed bin Qasim, who – allegedly provoked either by attacks on Muslim merchants who had either arrived in Sindh to buy female slaves, or on Arab ships carrying gifts to the Caliph in Damascus from the King of Ceylon – conquered the delta towns before marching upriver, terrifying the opposition with his rockets, as far as Multan. Arab dynasties ruled in the lower Indus for some two hundred years, becoming increasingly independent of the Abbasid and Ummayid dynasties in Damascus; but it was not until the early eleventh century that the rest of the Punjab was conquered for Islam by Mahmoud of Ghazni. This pattern of invasion from the north-west continued for the next 500 years – most notably by the Mongols, among them Genghis Khan and Timur, or Tamerlane – and culminated in Babur's victory at Paniput in 1526, and the establishment of the Moghul Empire, which ruled over the subcontinent from Lahore and later Delhi and Agra for the next 300 years.

The Indus is the backbone of Pakistan and the focal point of its history and of much of its culture; yet it has never been as navigable as the Nile or the Mississippi, or played as large a role in the trade and transport of the area. For much of its length, where it rushes through the mountains, it is far too fast and furious to be navigated with any degree of ease, and can only be forded or bridged at selected points. Below Kalabagh, where the river slows down and widens out, continual changes of course, sandbanks, shallow reaches and unsuspected currents and eddies make it a nightmare for the navigator; nor has the progress of shipping up the river been helped by the fact that the Indus has always stood in the way of, and been a prime target for, invading hordes on their way from Afghanistan and Central Asia to Delhi and central India. In the sixth century BC, one Scylax – a sailor employed by the emperor Darius of Persia – sailed the entire length of the Indus

The Manchar boat people use trained herons for fishing.
OVERLEAF *A typical Indus village near Kalabagh.*
Camels are used for transporting goods throughout the
Indus region

from Peshawar, on the tributary Kabul River, to the delta. Alexander the Great joined his admiral Nearchus and his fleet on the Jhelum before sailing slowly south, founding cities and fighting as they went, reaching the delta some nine months later; and during the first half of the nineteenth century the British, most notably in the colourful form of the traveller Alexander Burnes, made efforts to open up the lower reaches of the Indus to shipping, despite the fact that Burnes himself – taking with him horses and a carriage as a gift to the Sikh ruler, Ranjit Singh – had taken five months to reach Lahore in 1831, sailing when the wind allowed but otherwise being dragged upstream. Navigation was made no easier by the fact that the prevailing wind always follows the course of the river, setting up choppy waves in summer, when it blows from the south, and billowing clouds of sand in the winter, when it blows from the north. The introduction of railways by the British in the 1860s effectively put paid to the Indus in terms of long-distance freight and navigation, and the great dams and barrages that became a feature of the river during the first half of this century – providing hydroelectricity and irrigation, as well as controlling the supply of water during both the wet and dry seasons – provided the final nail in the coffin of long-distance water traffic on the Indus. Nowadays most of the traffic is essentially local, though the Indus fishermen continue to ply their trade – including the successors of those spotted by the Portuguese priest Sebastien Manrique in 1841, paddling to and fro balanced on large earthenware pots, which kept the fishermen afloat and at the same time trapped their prey.

The fact that the Indus is not a very navigable river is neither here nor there; far more worrying for the future of the area, by a cruel irony, are the side effects of irrigation and the network of canals which, sixty years ago, seemed to offer so much hope and prosperity to the Punjab and even to the desert wastes of Sindh. Below Kalbagh, the river suddenly slows down and broadens out; over the years it has moved across the plain, isolating once-important centres like Thatta and Mohenjodaro, the great city of the Indus Valley Civilisation, and overflowing its banks as the result of heavy floods caused by the

breaching of a dam upstream by earthquakes or the coincidence of the
monsoon with the period of the summer snow melt high up in the
Himalayas. For centuries, these flood waters were – whenever possible
– syphoned off into inundation canals, which were used for temporary
irrigation; but agriculture remained a precarious affair, in that an
adequate water supply could never be relied on all year round. In the
seventeenth century the emperor Jahangir built a canal from the Ravi
to a pleasure garden he had established on the other side of the river
from Lahore, and his son built another canal to irrigate the famous
Shalamir Gardens; but little was done until after the arrival of the
British, who took over Sindh in 1843 and the Punjab in 1849.

The British were eager to make the Punjab the granary of India,
and for this – they believed – a system of irrigation canals was essential.
The first permanent canal was opened in 1859; by 1900 the lower Indus

Practising at the Gymkhana Club ground, with the
Victorian Pavilion in the background.
OVERLEAF *Partridge shooting on the Nawab of*
Kalabagh's estate in the Salt Range, his private
bodyguards used as beaters (centre, Azam Khan, who was
at my school, Aitcheson College).

Basin was being considered as a whole, and the great rivers linked together by a network of canals. Adjustable barrages made it possible to build up reserves during the flood season for use in the dry season; they also helped to control flooding, as did protective walls, a system of observation points, and detailed hydrological records. In 1932 the Sukkur barrage opened, bringing into operation the greatest irrigation system in the world, and it was followed by a second barrage at Kalabagh in 1947. With Partition, it became impossible to deal with the region as a whole – India controlled the sources and the headwaters of many of Pakistan's rivers – but matters were improved by the Indus Basin Treaty of 1960, between India and Pakistan.

All this meant that two crops could now be relied upon every year, with farmers planting cotton, rice, maize, millet and sugar cane in the spring for harvesting in the autumn, and wheat, barley, grain and oil seeds in the autumn for harvesting in the spring. Settlements along the canals were encouraged by grants of land, and the peasants planted fields of cotton and wheat as well as citrus, mangoes, peaches and plums. But nothing is as simple as it seems, and the canals created their own unexpected problems of waterlogging and salinity. The trouble was that peasants tended to spread the water too generously, while the canals themselves were often unlined and therefore leaky; and the watertable began to rise, with disastrous results. As the water is drawn to the surface by the sun, it brings with it poisonous salts; when the water evaporates, these are left in the soil, killing off the crops and leaving whole stretches of the plains barren, white and sterile. Tube wells can be sunk, but they offer only a partial remedy; and in the Punjab – though not in Sindh – matters have been made worse by the failure of the irrigation engineers to provide drainage channels for excess water brought onto the fields. A recent Pakistan Economic Survey estimates that 9.5 million hectares of land are affected by waterlogging and salinity; within the Indus Basin, the watertable has risen to within six feet over 25 per cent of its area, and to within ten feet over a third of it, while 40,000 hectares are lost to agriculture every year. Nor are these the only problems: deforestation, especially in the foothills of the Himalayas, has led to massive soil erosion, with the monsoon rains carrying off the topsoil in once-wooded areas now short of vegetation. Many large dams – including those at Tarbela Mangla and Kalabagh – are situated in the foothills – and the reservoirs are being silted up by the eroded topsoil, particularly at Kalabagh. Not surprising, perhaps, severe flooding in the Indus Basin is much more frequent now than it was thirty years ago.

I have written at some length about these melancholy matters not only because they are of crucial importance to the future of Pakistan in general, and the Indus Valley in particular, but also because I feel so strongly about conservation. I feel desperately worried about the problems caused by the population explosion and by deforestation, and I intend to do everything I can to raise awareness of these problems. When I was at university in the early 1970s, I used to feel that socialism should be introduced into Pakistan, involving nationalisation, the redistribution of land, and the diminution of feudal landlords' holdings. But in the light of what has happened in Pakistan since, I have changed my mind completely. Nationalisation has been a complete disaster, with perfectly feasible industries running up huge losses overnight and leading to both corruption and high rates of inflation. The redistribution of land, which has been according to land productivity, has been equally disastrous, following the decision to set a ceiling on land holdings of fifty acres on fertile land. Land became unproductive, since farmers could no longer get the benefits of large-scale farming; but still worse were the effects on the environment.

The old feudal landlords tended to keep up game reserves – which meant maintaining forests and the wildlife which lived in them. As the landholdings have been reduced, so too have the forests and the wildlife. Shooting may well be a sport for the privileged few – but at least, paradoxically, it resulted in the country being richer in both forest cover and animal life. Of course the population explosion has not helped, but as I travelled round the country I couldn't help noticing that the best maintained areas were those in which large estates had managed to survive. In Sindh, for example, the feudal landlords have

not been as badly hit as their equivalents in the Punjab, with the result that there is plenty of game as well as some surviving forests. By far the most successful estate in Punjab belongs to the Nawab of Kalabagh: not only does he practise excellent modern farming methods, which are commercially extremely successful, but he also has a game reserve which is teeming with wildlife. The reserve is guarded by his private army, and poachers run a far greater risk than the animals they seek to poach. I fear that in the future game reserves may well have to be defended by well-trained guards. Since the Afghan War the country has been flooded with sophisticated weapons, which can be easily and cheaply obtained – and provide one of the reasons why wildlife in accessible areas has been virtually eliminated.

The enormous population explosion in the years since Partition – from 40 million to the present 110 million – has meant that the Government has not been able to devote sufficient resources to health, education, the preservation of the environment and the maintenance of historical monuments. Our health services have actually deteriorated since 1947, as has our education system; our literacy rate has actually fallen – something in which we must be almost unique.

My suggestion to the Pakistani Government is that it should thoroughly reduce government control in the country. Certainly the economy should be freed as far as possible of bureaucratic controls: our people have so much go and initiative, but they are strangled at every stage by red tape. And since salaries have been left far behind the rate of inflation, government controls merely lead to more corruption – and it's hard to blame badly paid government servants, unable to support their families on their meagre salaries.

When I was a child we used to spend our summer holidays either in Ghora Ghali, which is about 25 miles from Islamabad, or in Murree,

Keeping fit in Baltistan with my teammate, Zakir Khan.
OVERLEAF *Crossing a tributary of the Indus in the Swat Valley.*

a hill resort which had been developed by the British – eager, as we were, to escape the heat of summer on the plains and in Lahore. Murree is in the foothills of the Himalayas, 7000 feet up, in the kind of country that is now being threatened by deforestation. Quite apart from the cool mountain air, which grew cooler the higher we climbed up from the hot, dusty plains, and the bright, crystal-clear climate, what I remember best as we trekked and climbed in the hills was the wildlife: monkeys, jackals, foxes, and hundreds of exotic birds. Like everywhere else, Murree is more crowded now than it was in the 1960s; but it remains a magical spot despite losing some of its trees and the resulting landslides, and I only hope that future generations will be able to enjoy it as I did.

When I was about seven years old my parents took us to a rest home for our summer holidays, a few miles above Murree in a place called Doonga Gali. I'll never forget the commotion caused throughout the area when a panther killed a donkey next to our rest house. The excitement grew even greater when hunters came in from the sur-rounding countryside and built *machans* (camouflaged platforms) around the kill: luckily the crafty panther sensed trouble and failed to show up. Quite recently a panther made its way into someone's garage in Islamabad, which is about forty miles from Doonga Gali. The police were called, and some forty bullets were pumped into the unfortunate animal. When the news broke next day, the police action was widely condemned; with the result that when a month or so later, a snow leopard walked into someone's house way up in Chitral, in the Kara-koram, an expert was flown in from Karachi to dart the leopard with a sedative before letting it back into the wild.

I also got to know the interior of Pakistan through my passion for shooting – which is perfectly compatible, it seems to me, with my strong feelings about the preservation of our wildlife. My mother's family in particular were mad about shooting; and her brother, my uncle Ahmad Raza Khan, used to take me to shoots when I was only six or seven years old. We'd camp out or stay in one of those wonderfully isolated rest houses in the middle of nowhere. Very often we went to the Salt Range, which has remained my favourite place for shooting. The Salt Range is a ridge that runs some hundred miles from the Chenab – one of the five tributaries of the Indus that give the Punjab its name – to the Indus itself. Perhaps because of its high salt content, it is teeming with wildlife.

In the early sixteenth century the Emperor Babur – who invaded India from Afghanistan, and established the great Moghul dynasty which ruled the sub-continent until the last century – used to hunt rhinos in the Salt Range: those days are long gone, alas, but one can still hunt the huryal, a kind of mountain sheep, as well as varieties of partridge, the sisi (like the french partridge), the chakor and, along the banks of rivers and streams, the black partridge. Although I'd like to see some of the larger forms of game conserved, I've always enormously enjoyed shooting partridge, provided it's done within the spirit of the sport; and, like grouse in England, they tend to die from disease if their numbers go above a certain level.

In the 1950s my uncle Ahmad Raza Khan was the Deputy Commissioner of Jhelum, a town in the Salt Range on the banks of the River Jhelum. One day some villagers found a female leopard cub, and presented it to him; and he brought it back to Zaman Park, our home in Lahore where my mother's family had settled after Partition. I have vague childhood memories of the cub – not least that all the dogs within a quarter of a mile radius of the house were absolutely terrified of it. After about the age of four months it had to be chained up: one day, a rather bold German Shepherd ventured too close, only to have a strip of its coat removed with a single swipe of the leopard's claws. Eventually my uncle had to donate it to the Lahore Zoo, where it grew into a very large and beautiful adult leopard.

My uncle ran his shoots in a fairly lavish way; he was very correct about observing the codes for shooting. He'd invite his sons, his nephews and all his friends for two days and two nights, and we'd have a marvellous time, with huge feasts at lunchtime and at night. Winters in Pakistan are perfect for this kind of thing; in fact, I don't know of any country that has winters to match. At night it's extremely cold, so that we used to sit round log fires, listening to the jackals and other animals calling in the wilderness; it's misty and cold in the early morning, but once the mist has cleared one gets the most beautiful sunny days, and can walk round in shirtsleeves. Sometimes, at night, we'd shoot wild boar from jeeps: boar tend to destroy crops, and the government actually pays a bounty to anyone who shoots them.

Mention of my uncle raises the subject of my family. Although I grew up in Lahore, my father's family village, Mianwali, is on the Indus. His tribe, the Niazi, were Pathans who came to India from Afghanistan in the thirteenth or fourteenth century. Later on they helped the Lodhi Sultans to rule India from Delhi – the Lodhis were a sister tribe, and Bal Lodhi issued a *firman* or order to the effect that the Pathan tribes should help him to rule India, since there were too few Pathans in India at the time, and it was an enormous country to govern. Lodhi rule came to an end when Babur defeated the Sultan's army at the first Battle of Paniput in 1526, but the Niazis were again to the fore when my great hero Sher Shah Suri deposed Babur's son, the Emperor Humayun, in 1540. I'll have more to say about him when I come to describe the fort at Rohtas, on the Kahan river. An ancestor of mine, Haibat Khan Niazi, was one of Sher Shah Suri's leading generals, as well as being the governor of Punjab. One of the problems with Pathans is that they find it almost impossible not to feud amongst themselves. Fighting broke out among Sher Shah Suri's successors after his death: Haibat Khan backed the wrong side in the civil war and was killed, and the restoration of Moghul rule under Humayun – who had been in exile in Iran – marked the end of Niazi political power or influence.

And yet the Niazis are only one strand among many in the rich pattern of Pakistani life and culture. As my text, and Mike Goldwater's magnificent photographs will, I hope, make clear, Pakistan is a country with a stunning variety of scenery, peoples and ways of life, and the best possible introduction to it is to follow upstream the course of the Indus, the mighty 'lion river'.

Explaining cricket to a small Baltistani boy.

PART 1

Sindh

We began our journey in the far south, in the dry, flat plains of Sindh. Best-remembered (to English readers at least) for General Napier's telegraphic pun announcing its annexation by the British in 1843 ('I have Sind'), it derives its name, 'Sindhu', from the Indus; yet much of it remained desert, which may well have accounted for its having been rather cut off from the rest of the sub-continent until comparatively recent times. It was incorporated into the Persian Empire by Darius I; after Alexander the Great had passed through with his fleet, sailing

down the Indus en route for the delta and the sea beyond, it was successively ruled by Greeks, Hindus, Indo-Greeks and Scythians. Under the Kushana Emperor Kanishka it was, for a short time, a Buddhist principality; but it was being ruled by the Hindu Brahmans when Muhammed bin Qasim led his Arab invasion in 711 AD, his forces including six thousand Syrian horsemen, a camel corps and stone-throwing catapults. Sad to say, Qasim came to a sticky end. He sent back to the Caliph in Baghdad two of the Rajah's beautiful daughters, one of whom complained on arrival – unjustly, it turned out – that Qasim had slept with them before dispatching them home; the Caliph was so incensed by this piece of *lèse-majesté* that he ordered Qasim to be flayed alive and his body, stuffed with straw, was shipped back to Damascus in disgrace.

Although the power of the remote Ummayid and Abbasid dynasties in the Middle East inevitably waned over the years, Arab dynasties ruled in Sindh until 1026, when the Turkoman Mahmoud of Ghazni – Ghazni is a town in Afghanistan – captured Multan in the Punjab before moving south to take Sindh as well. Like so much of the Indus Valley, Sindh was invaded and ravaged again and again by, in particular, the Mongols: Timur, or Tamerlane, passed through on his way to Delhi in the late fourteenth century, and from 1591 to 1700 the province came under what proved to be – thanks to its remoteness from Delhi – very loose Moghul rule. During the eighteenth century the Persian King, Nadir Shah, took most of Sindh from the Moghuls, whose power was now in very evident decline; it was then ruled, for a time, from Afghanistan by the Kalhora Mirs (or Emirs) until they in turn were overthrown by the Talpur Mirs in 1782.

Europeans first set foot in Sindh in the sixteenth century in the form of the Portuguese, who founded churches and set up trading posts. But both the Kalhora and the Talpur Mirs were keen to keep out

A Sindhi villager.
PREVIOUS PAGES: LEFT *Thatta, the Shah Jehan Mosque.* ABOVE *Fisherman on Lake Manchar.*

29

European intruders, with the result that the East India Company – which ruled so much of British India until after the Mutiny – failed to get a firm foothold in the eighteenth century.

But the British proved too strong, and too persistent, for the Mirs. A British mission to the Talpur Mirs in Hyderabad in 1809 provided a foot in the door, and by 1820 the Mirs had agreed to allow no other Europeans to settle in Sindh. The rise of Ranjit Singh's powerful Sikh Empire in the Punjab in the early years of the nineteenth century provided the British with an ideal opportunity to improve their standing. They offered to protect Sindh against the Sikhs, and British troops were stationed in the province. Matters were made worse by doomed British attempts to open the Indus to navigation: the Mirs' traditional hunting grounds along the Indus were destroyed in order to provide fuel for the flat-bottomed river steamers which picked their way slowly upstream, at the mercy of sandbanks, currents and ever-changing

Wheat harvest in Sindh.

30

contours of the river. Resentment rose in the Sindh, and rebellion broke out after the British had become involved in the disastrous First Afghan War: but the Mirs' Baluchi army was routed by Sir Charles Napier at the Battle of Miani in 1843, losing five thousand men against Napier's 257. British firepower had won the day against a courageous but ill-equipped enemy: as Napier later confessed, 'We have no right to seize Sindh, yet we shall do so, and a very advantageous, humane and useful piece of rascality it will be.' Nor was Napier entirely cynical. One of his first priorities was to set up a Canal Department, and in 1855 Colonel Fife produced a report on providing canals for the entire province. Within fifty years Sindh had been transformed, and its production of cotton, maize, wheat, rice, sugar cane, corn, millet, oil seed, mangoes, bananas and dates put farming on a new footing, with 38% of the land area under active cultivation. Since 1947, the

Meerbahars on the Manchar.
OVERLEAF *Ancient necropolis at Makli, near Thatta.*

population of Sindh doubled, the greatest density being in the cities. Karachi, the former capital of Pakistan and now the capital of Sindh Province, is by far the largest city, not only in Sindh, but in the whole of the Indus Valley.

According to the mid nineteenth-century British traveller and reprobate, Hugo James, 'the Sindee is a fine, tall and handsome man, with a dark complexion.' Unfortunately, James doesn't make it clear whether he is talking about the Sindhis or the Baluchis. The Sindhis are an altogether more settled people than the Baluchis – who are not dissimilar to my own people, the Pathans. According to one tradition the Baluchis can be traced back to Aleppo in Syria – though another legend has it that they are the Chaldean descendants of Beleus, the Babylonian king Nimrod. The Baluchis are organised in tribes, and each *qabilah* (tribe) or *qawm* (community) is headed by a *sardar* or *khan*; as with the Pathans, the *jirgah* – specific to each community – serves

Stone carvings at the Makli Necropolis.

34

as an unwritten law and as a judicial tribunal. *Mayar* or *nang* is the traditional Baluchi code of honour, based on chivalry and the blood feud; Baluchis tend to marry as closely within the family as possible to prevent blood feuds – maybe in this respect they're less addicted to feuding than their compatriots to the north! They're fond of wrestling, of fairs, of horse and camel races and of falconry; according to the British Government Gazetteer of 1874, 'So great was their love for their *shikargahs*, or hunting enclosures, that they are said to have declared they value them as much as their wives and children.' Since then these traditionally nomadic people have become increasingly urbanised, but no doubt a germ of truth remains . . .

Like the Pathans, the Baluchis are essentially a mountain people, who, because of the hard conditions in the hills of Eastern Sindh, raided the plains and, in some cases, settled there as well. In southern

A watch tower at Pir Patho, near Thatta, beside the old river bed.

35

Sindh Baluchi influence is far slighter, but to the north the Baluchis provided what was, in effect, a ruling class; and although, over the years, the Sindhis and the Baluchis have intermarried to some extent, they continue to speak different languages and to look very different. Baluchistan remains the least inhabited and least explored part of Pakistan. The northern areas were occupied by the British and therefore exposed to influences from the outside world, but large areas in the south that belonged to the Kalat State remained unexplored and very fascinating. I remember how, a few years back, I took some friends from England to a shoot about six hours' drive into the interior from Fort Munroe. (Baluchistan has some of the best *chukor* (a plump game bird) shooting in Pakistan, though such occasions are hard to organise. Over 'Christmas camp' the British Army used to organise massive *chukor* shoots.) When we got to our destination – an isolated fort in the middle of nowhere – we were woken in the middle of the night by the army police. They told us that army intelligence had learned of a plan by Baluchi tribesmen to kidnap and hold to ransom a group of foreigners who were in the area – the Government would be held responsible for the safety of any foreigners, and would be expected to pay the ransom. Some tribes still live by robbing and kidnapping – conditions are so hard, and the land so unproductive. Certainly it's a part of the country I would love to explore in more detail: the area round Fort Munroe struck me as being extremely wild, yet it is supposed to be relatively civilised!

The first town on our itinerary was Thatta. A centre of Muslim power and learning from the fourteenth to the eighteenth centuries, it is now – despite its magnificent buildings and its former glory – little more than, in Jean Fairley's words, 'a large and dilapidated village'; for the Indus, which provided it with its raison d'etre, has changed its course and is now six miles away, leaving Thatta stranded. Although Alexander the Great is said to have rested his troops there while his admiral, Nearchus, assembled the fleet in the Indus delta for the long

Dervish dances at the Mausoleum of Lal Shahbaz Qalandar.

36

journey home, Thatta was, according to legend, founded by the Samma prince, Jam Nizam-ud-din, who is buried in the enormous necropolis outside the town at Makli Hill. Thatta developed as a river port, trading in silk and cotton goods. In 1555 it was burned and pillaged by Portuguese mercenaries, who had sailed up the Indus in twenty-eight pinnaces after being summoned (unwisely, as it turned out) by the then ruler of Sindh to help him against his enemies; and it was destroyed again in 1592, when the Moghul Emperor Akbar invaded Sindh.

During the sixteenth century, Thatta was incorporated into the Moghul Empire. In 1644 the Emperor Shah Jehan began work on the famous mosque that bears his name – he was very attached to Thatta, taking refuge there during the struggle that followed the death of his father, and built the mosque in gratitude.

Women reciting the Holy Quran at Sehwan.
OVERLEAF *Fishermen on Lake Manchar.*

Despite the ravages of its own special form of plague or fever – the 1908 *Gazetteer* describes it as a 'feverish spot', and notes that British troops often suffered the ill effects of its 'stagnant pools and unwholesome water' – Thatta was a large town by the end of the seventeenth century; yet even then a contemporary European visitor noted that although 'linen calicuts' made in Multan, in the Punjab, were being shipped down-river for sale in Thatta, the channel of the Indus was 'spoiled' and its mouth 'quite stopped up with sands'. Its population began to decline during the eighteenth century, and by the time Alexander Burnes visited Thatta in 1831 it was down to 10,000; according to Burnes, 'it is deemed throughout Sinde one of the lowest and most unhealthy sites'. As we have seen, Burnes (and the British in general) were keen to open up the Indus to navigation, and by 1840 four iron paddle-steamers were operating on the lower Indus, taking eight days to make the journey from Thatta to Sukkur. A year or two later the pleasure-loving Hugo James came to Thatta, which – he claimed – had 'the stigma of being the most licentious city in the universe'. He also noted that 'scattered round the suburbs and within the precincts of the town are several handsome tombs, mosques and buildings, but all fast going to decay' – a reference to the vast necropolis of sandstone monuments at Makli Hill. This extraordinary place is well worth a visit; jewellery on a monument indicates a woman's grave, a knight on horseback a man's. Sad to say, many of the wonderful tombs have been vandalised, with some of the most beautiful stonework lying in the drawing-rooms of well-to-do people in Karachi. I cannot see matters improving, since the guards on the necropolis are so poor and so easy to bribe.

Upstream from Thatta is the town of Sehwan. According to legend, Alexander the Great was wounded by an arrow while besieging Sehwan on his way down the Indus to the delta. Sehwan was then a Malli fortress: the Malli may well have been a people of Dravidian origin, similar to those who now live by Lake Manchnar, fishing and wild-fowling. The Dravidians were the original inhabitants of the sub-continent, who were subjugated or driven away by the invading

Aryans in the second millennium B C; apart from isolated pockets, most of their descendants are now found in southern India. Sehwan boasts a fort called Sikandar-ko-jillo, a mound some 80–90 feet high: despite its evocative name – 'Sikandar' is a common adaptation of Alexander – it has nothing to do with the Macedonian invader. Sehwan may once have been the capital of the Samma people; as at Thatta, the river has moved away and left it stranded. But for me the most interesting thing about Sehwan is the tomb of Shahbaz Qalandar, one of the greatest Muslim saints of Sindh. Certainly he seems to have been blessed with extraordinary powers. We stayed at the government rest house, which had been built some seventy years ago by the British. This rest house is on the site of the old fort; and from this fort, at the time of the Great Sufi, there once ruled a Rajah called Cherbut. Cherbut was widely known for his cruelty, and he employed as his excecutioner someone called Anood Kasair – 'kasai' meaning butcher. Shahbaz Qalandar sent messages to the Rajah, begging him to go easy on the townspeople. Eventually he sent an emissary called Bodla Barbar, who was – quite literally – cut to pieces by Anood the butcher; yet no sooner had he been cut up than he was miraculously put together again. This happened seven times; when Shahbaz Qalandar eventually learned what was happening to his emissary he waved his staff, the entire fort was turned upside down, and everyone in it – including the wicked Rajah and his butcher – was killed. According to legend, since then no one has ever been able to dig in the fort. People have tried to excavate in the fort, but without any luck; and those who have tried have been haunted by bad dreams or even died suddenly in the night. Not surprisingly, all excavations of the fort have eventually been abandoned. According to another tradition, it's almost impossible for thieves to commit robberies in Sehwan: they always get caught in the act.

Sufism made an early appearance in Sindh and the Punjab. One of the first Sufis to reach the sub-continent was Sheikh Ismail from

A Sindhi milk carrier.

Suhrawardi, was even elected King of Multan and northern Sindh, though his reign was short-lived.

Twelve Sufi sects have been mentioned by Al-Hajwiri: Hululi, Hullaji, Tayfuri, Qussari, Khariaji, Khafifi, Sayyari, Muhasibi, Tustari, Hakimi, Nari and Junaydi. Sufis have made a remarkable literary contribution as well: many of the major poets of Punjabi and Sindhi were great Sufis, including Baba Fareed, Sultan Bahu, Shah Hussain, Khawaja Fareed, Sachal Sarmast, Shahbaz Qalandar and Shah Abdul Lateef Bhitai.

The Indus has been up to its tricks once again at Mohenjodaro, to the north of Sehwan; indeed, this may have been one of the reasons for the sudden and mysterious end of what was, for at least a thousand years, the most impressive city of the Indus Valley Civilisation. Until early in this century, no one had ever even suspected the existence of this highly sophisticated pre-Aryan culture, which covered a far larger area than its contemporaries in Egypt and Mesopotamia, and was quite their equal in terms of buildings, artefacts and standards of living. As far as we know, the Indus Valley Civilisation flourished between

Ruins of the Great Bath at the ancient city of Mohenjodaro.

approximately 2500 and 1500 BC; it covered an area of more than a thousand miles in length, and produced a culture of extraordinary uniformity in terms of both time and distance. The city of Harappa, in the Punjab, was discovered in 1862, and excavated in the 1920s by Sir John Marshall, who had an important role in excavating the far larger, and finer, city of Mohenjodaro. In 1944, Lord Wavell – the then Governor-General of India – appointed the well-known British archaeologist Sir Mortimer Wheeler to be his Director-General of Archaeology; and in 1950 Wheeler also began to work on the excavation of Mohenjodaro. According to the historian Gordon Childe, both Harappa and Mohenjodaro were 'vast, orderly and populous cities'; Mohenjodaro itself was unfortified, and was essentially a trading city. The 'upper city' was raised up, and probably contained the citadel, and the centres of religious and civic administration; while – as the visitor can easily see for himself – the 'lower city' was laid out in a rectangular grid pattern. Prosperous merchants lived in two-storeyed houses, made from fine, lightly-fired bricks, and often built round a courtyard. Like the ancient Romans, the inhabitants of Mohenjodaro appeared to have paid great attention to drainage and sanitation; many houses had baths, sit-down lavatories and brick-covered drains. Sewage was either stored in brick-lined soil tanks or large pottery jars, which were collected by municipal 'sanitary squads', while rubbish chutes appear to have been a standard feature of many houses. The city's huge granaries were ventilated by grids and air ducts.

Not only are the artefacts found at Mohenjodaro very similar to those from Mesopotamia – suggesting trade between these two river-based civilisations – but Babylonian and Dravidian myths have much in common. No one quite knows what form religion took in the Indus Valley Civilisation, and no evidence of religious buildings or temples has been found at Mohenjodaro, but mother goddess figurines have been discovered. The pictographic writing has yet to be deciphered.

Equally baffling are the reasons for Mohenjodaro's sudden decline. Mortimer Wheeler thought the city had been destroyed by 'mobile,

Aror: This extraordinary rock formation was a famous hiding place of dacoits (bandits) during the British Raj.

cityless invaders' – in other words, the Aryans, pouring out of Central Asia over the North-West Frontier – yet there is no evidence in the remains of battle or destruction. Or could it be – as has happened so often elsewhere – that the life-giving river moved away, and the irrigation systems fell into disuse and decay?

Further upstream, but still within Sindh, are the towns of Khairpur and Rohri, and the great barrage at Sukkur. Khairpur is situated on the great alluvial plain: away from the river, the country is arid and sterile, the home of hyenas, jackals, foxes, wild hogs, deer, gazelle and antelope, and of bustards, wild geese, snipe and partridge. The bustard, now a rare bird, used to abound in profusion in Sindh and the Southern Punjab. Large-scale poaching by the army and massive hunting operations by Arabs from all over the Middle East has virtually led to its extinction. However, some Arab princes now have well-guarded reserves which have given the bird some protection. But

The British-built barrage at Sukkur.

unless the government steps in, it looks as if the imperial bustard will disappear.

Early in the last century Khairpur came under the rule of the Talpur Mirs of Sindh, the three separate and rival dynasties which were based on Hyderabad, Mirpur and Khairpur (these family divisions were exacerbated by some members being Sunni Moslems, and others Shia). The jealousy between two Talpur brothers led to British intervention and, in 1832, to a treaty with Khairpur State whereby use of the Indus and roads within Sindh were secured to the British. The other Sindh Mirs were reluctant to go along with this, but the Khairpur Mir was allowed a far greater degree of independence by the British as a reward for his co-operation. Hugo James, opinionated as ever, seems to have had a low opinion of both the Mir and his city, chastising the Mir as

Elaborate ceramic and stone carvings at the Moghul
graveyards overlooking the Indus.
OVERLEAF *Unloading watermelons at Sukkur.*

an unfeeling tyrant over-fond of champagne breakfasts, while Khairpur itself was 'disgustingly dirty and badly built; dead animals are allowed to remain for days in public thoroughfares . . .' Mind you, much British writing of the time was extremely racist: they were self-righteous, and usually had a low opinion of other races.

The town of Rohri is set on a limestone cliff on the left bank of the Indus. It is said to have been founded by Syed Rukn-ud-din in 1297, but is best known for the Nur Mubarak Mosque, which was built in 1745, by Nur Mohammed, the reigning Kalkhora Mir, to house a hair from the beard of the Prophet, which was attributed with miraculous powers and enclosed in a gold case studded with rubies and emeralds; it used to be exposed to view every March, and was said to rise and fall as well as changing colour.

Sukkur is the site of the first great barrage to be built by the British. It is situated on a low limestone ridge – the country round about is rocky, with little vegetation – and the barrage was built where the Indus runs through a gorge in the limestone cliffs. The river forms a lake behind the barrage: Sukkur has become something of a port, with cargo and fishing boats tied up at the quay, and – as elsewhere along the Lower Indus – the river and fishing peoples lead their own fiercely independent lives, living in houseboats or in thatched wooden huts perched over the water.

Sukkur was ceded 'in perpetuity' to the British in 1842, and rapidly developed as a garrison town, with a chain of forts protecting the Area and British officers enjoying the delights of pig-sticking and tiger shooting. The British in general found it unhealthy and unbearably hot; they complained that the fish from the river were not worth eating – according to Hugo James – having 'little flavour, and an inconvenient quantity of bones', while Sukkur itself was 'a ruined city, entire streets of houses having fallen to decay'.

A young Sindhi girl making models from Indus clay.

PART 2

The Punjab

Whereas Sindh – or at least that part of it through which the Indus flows – is uniformly flat and dry, Punjab, the province to its north, offers a far greater variety of landscape, from the beautiful Vale of Kashmir and the foothills of the Himalayas to the arid desert of the south. 'Punjab' means 'five waters' – a reference to the five great tributaries of the Indus – the Jhelum, the Chenab, the Ravi, the Beas and the Sutlej – that run through the middle of the province, and give it much of its character.

Like Sindh, the Punjab was annexed onto

the Persian Empire in about 518 BC. After Alexander the Great had passed through, the Punjab was absorbed into the Mauryan Empire of Chandragupta; under his grandson, Ashoka, the Buddhist Mauryan dynasty controlled an area that stretched from the Sutlej to the Hindu Kush. Nearly a thousand years later, in 712 AD, the Arabs conquered the lower Punjab; but it was not until the eleventh century that the rest of the Punjab was claimed for Islam by Mahmoud of Ghazni. In 1206 the Punjab came, for the first time, under the control of the Sultanate at Delhi, and was ruled by, in succession, Khaljis, Tughluqs, Sayyids, and from 1451 to 1526 Pathan Lodhis. Unfortunately the Pathans were incapable of co-operating amongst themselves; Babur, the first Moghul Emperor, was asked by one faction to intervene, and promptly assumed power in Lahore and then in Delhi. By the eighteenth century Moghul power was waning throughout India, and the Punjab fell to an Afghan tribe, the Durranis, ruling from Kabul; but by the end of the century a new power had arisen in the Punjab, that was to present the British with their most formidable adversary yet.

The Sikh religion was established in the fifteenth century by Guru Nanak, and the Sikhs themselves are instantly recognisable by their turbans and beards, and by the fact that male Sikhs are never supposed to shave or cut their hair. Ranjit Singh, 'the lion of the Punjab', was the greatest of all Sikh leaders. In 1799 he captured Lahore from the Durranis, and two years later proclaimed himself the Maharajah of the Punjab; he captured Multan in 1818, and Kashmir the following year. He defeated the Pathans and the Afghans; annexed the remote provinces of Baltistan and Ladakh, high in the mountains between the Himalayas and the Karakoram, near the source of the Indus; and extended Sikh power to the Khyber Pass. According to the early

PREVIOUS PAGES: LEFT *Pumping water in the Cholistan Desert near Uch.*
ABOVE *My friend Yousaf entertaining at his* havelli *in the Old City of Lahore.*

nineteenth-century traveller Emily Eden, Ranjit looked 'exactly like an old mouse with grey whiskers and one eye', while the French explorer Jacqument called him 'my beloved Maharajah'. Almost a dwarf, with a pockmarked face and slurred speech, he was addicted to horses, drink, opium and women. He was also a very great soldier, and a consummate politician. Sikhism is in itself a military creed, and Punjabis of all faiths are well-known as soldiers; Ranjit harnessed this martial spirit, and united the leading Sikh families in a sense of national unity. He also made shrewd use of French and Italian mercenaries, such as the Neapolitan soldier of fortune, Avitabile, later the governor of Peshawar. Apart from establishing a powerful if short-lived empire, Ranjit amassed a personal fortune that included the most famous diamond in the world, the Koh-i-noor, which was captured by the

The Jewanti Tomb at Uch. The man in the foreground is digging a grave.

59

British after the Second Sikh War and presented to Queen Victoria. But the British trod warily as long as Ranjit himself was alive: in 1831 Alexander Burnes – the explorer and adventurer who had been so keen to open up the Indus to navigation, and who was eventually to lose his life in the First Afghan War – arrived at his court with a present of horses, and a coach lined with blue velvet.

In 1839 Ranjit died, and his empire began to fall apart. The First Sikh War of 1845–6 was followed two years later by the Second Sikh War; as a result of their own folly, the Sikhs were finally defeated at the battles of Gujrat and Chilianwala, and the entire Punjab was annexed by the British.

The town of Uch is situated on the south bank of the Sutlej, near its confluence with the Chenab; Alexander the Great was much given to founding as well as besieging cities on his way down the Indus, and Uch has – rightly or wrongly – been identified as one of these. In the twelfth century it was known as 'Deogarh' or 'the gods' stronghold'. According to legend, its ruler, Deo Singh, fled at the arrival of the Muslim saint and missionary, Syed Jalal-ud-din – who then proceeded to convert Deo Singh's daughter, Sundarpuri, to Islam, and told her to build a fort called 'uccha' or 'ucch', meaning 'high' or 'high place'. Uch became a centre of Muslim learning, and in 1227 the celebrated Persian historian Minhaj-ud-din was made principal of Firoz College; although now a small town, it has had an enormous influence on the religious life of this part of the world. The oldest shrine in the city is that of Sheikh Saif-ud-din Ghazrooni, who was probably the first Muslim saint to settle in Uch; his tomb may well be the oldest Moslem tomb in the entire sub-continent. As soon as one arrives in Uch, one is aware of the weight of history – and of the fact that the town has been decaying for several centuries.

At Dera Naub, just to the south of Bahawalpur, we paid a visit to the palace belonging to the princes Salahuddin and Falahuddin, both

PREVIOUS PAGE *Life in the Cholistan Desert, where* (RIGHT) *this woman lives.*

62

of whom had been at school with me – it is, in fact, the private residence of the Nawab of Bahawalpur. I was very upset by the poor state of the palace. Whereas in India the great maharajahs' palaces are, more often than not, very well looked after, this is far from being the case in Pakistan; and I do feel very strongly that the government should make money available to restore and maintain these marvellous buildings. The former rulers no longer have the necessary funds, but perhaps they could be turned into luxury hotels rather than crumble into ruins.

Much of the same applies to the palace of the Nawab of Bahawalpur. Under the British, Bahawalpur was far and away the biggest state in what was later to become Pakistan. It was a princely state; the Nawab

ABOVE *The dilapidated Dera Nawab Palace at Bahawalpur.*
RIGHT *Nawab Falahuddin beneath a painting of the Battle of Waterloo.*

owned three palaces, and was one of only five princely rulers through-out the whole of India to be entitled to a twenty-five gun salute. One reason for this was that the Nawab had always been on excellent terms with the British. When Ranjit Singh rose to power in the Punjab, the then Nawab appealed to the British for protection, and in 1833 a treaty between the Nawab and the British opened up that stretch of the Indus and the Sutlej to river traffic. During the first Afghan War (1839–1843) the Nawab furnished supplies to the British and facilitated the passage of troops on their way through to Afghanistan; he co-operated with Sir Herbert Edwardes over the Multan campaign, during the Second Sikh War; and some thirty years later we find the then Nawab placing his entire resources at the disposal of the British.

The palace in Bahawalpur itself was built in 1882 to designs by a European architect. It's a very beautiful building, and it has one of two curious stories attached to it. There is a pond outside the palace which became infested with crocodiles after one or two had come in through the canals: getting rid of them proved a nightmarish business, involving nets and, sad to say, the loss of several limbs. Until very recently the Nawab lived in amazing style and grandeur: when Mr Bhutto was Prime Minister, in 1974, he asked the Nawab to accommodate and cater for seven thousand people at a fortnight's notice – and the Nawab obliged without a second thought. Until about fifty years ago the Nawab had a marvellous game reserve in a forest, where he could take his guests tiger-shooting – but the forests have all been destroyed since then.

Few places in Pakistan have had a more dramatic history than Multan, which is situated on a wedge of land enclosed by the Chenab and the Sutlej. The country round about is often flooded in summer: the British used to say that no other place in the sub-continent boasted such consistently high temperatures, and the city itself was renowned for its heat and dust, and for the intensity of its dust storms. According to a local legend, a saint who was being flayed alive called on the sun to avenge him, with the result that the sun is closer to Multan than to any other place on earth.

Another local legend claims that Multan is as old as the Flood, and that Yafis – a son of Noah – settled there once the waters had receded. Be that as it may, Multan has been identified with the Kaspaeria mentioned by Ptolemy, the Greek geographer; and it may well have been known first as Kasyapapura, named after Kasypa, the father of Adityas and Daityas, the sun gods and titans of Hindu mythology. It was almost certainly the major city of the Malli, whom Alexander the Great defeated after stiff opposition. When Alexander moved on he left Philippius as his satrap, but Multan quickly fell under the rule of the Mauryan dynasty. They were followed in turn by the Bactrian Greeks – Greek coins have been discovered in the city – and then by a long period of Buddhist domination. The famous Chinese traveller Hieun Tsiang, to whom we owe so much of our knowledge of the period, came to Multan in 641 AD, and described a gorgeously attired gold idol, an image of the sun, in the chief temple of the town.

The interior of the Leghari House at Choti.

In 712 AD Multan fell to the Arabs under Qasim, but by 900 AD its governor was, in effect, independent of Baghdad. For the next three centuries or so it lay in the direct line of the Mongol invasions, and was repeatedly sacked. In 1528 Babur annexed Multan province into his empire; and the last of the great Moghul emperors, Aurangzeb, finally destroyed the temple of the sun and replaced it with a mosque.

One of the most dramatic incidents in the history of Multan occurred in 1848, when the murder of the two British officers triggered off the Second Sikh War. Ranjit Singh had captured and sacked Multan in 1818, but after his death British power and influence in the area had steadily increased. This was matched by increasing discontent among the Sikhs, which came to a head when Mulraj, the governor of Multan, proved unable to pay any taxes after Henry Lawrence had abolished the duty on river-borne goods. Two British officers, Vans Agnew and Anderson, were sent to Multan to remonstrate with Mulraj; they were attacked by the townspeople, and although Herbert Edwardes eventually managed to bring his troops into Multan from the other side of the river – there was no bridge, and crossing the Indus and its tributaries is seldom an easy business – both men had been killed by the time he arrived.

Multan itself is built on a mound, formed from the debris of former cities; the main city is still walled, with six gates. Multan is not only one of the earliest Islamic towns in the Punjab, but it boasts a larger number of saints, mystics and divines, and more tombs in one place, than anywhere else in Pakistan. The city is dominated by the red-brick and marble shrine of its eleventh-century patron saint, Shah Rukn-e-Alam – a magnificent octagonal building over a hundred feet high – which is an object of veneration not only to Pakistanis but to pilgrims from all parts of the Muslim word. One thing is certain: excavations could reveal a very great deal at Multan.

Religious festivals in Multan are a peculiar mixture of devotion and merriment. Multan is famous for its innumerable shrines, and once a year homage is paid to each departed saint: the ceremony usually lasts three days, with the first day given over to prayer and exhibitions of

physical prowess, and the remaining two to merry-making. One of the best-known saints of Multan was Hazrat Bahauddin Zakaria, who was born in 1182. After visiting Baghdad, Medina, Bukhara and Jerusalem, he founded a university at Multan, which became famous throughout India, Arabia and the Middle East. His mausoleum is decorated in the blue tiles that are a speciality of Multan – as are the hand-painted vases and plates. Equally well-known is the tomb of Shamsuddin Sabzwari, the saint who is said to have caused the sun to come closer to Multan than anywhere else. According to another story, this particular saint, while on a visit to Baghdad, willed back to life the dead son of the Caliph. For some reason, this upset the local mullahs, who urged that he should be skinned alive; when the saint learned of this he presented them with his entire skin, and set off back to India.

The intricate decoration within the Leghari house is in need of restoration.

Under the Emperor Aurangzeb, Lahore began to decline in population and importance: the Emperor preferred to spend more time in Delhi, and the trappings of power drifted away to the east. Nor did Aurangzeb help the cause of Lahore by building embankments along the Ravi to control flooding: they were only too successful, with the result that the river, fickle as ever, changed course and moved away. He did, however, build the Badshahi Mosque in Lahore – one of the largest in the world – in 1664.

Not much more than a century later, however, Lahore was once again a capital city – this time of the short-lived Sikh Empire of Ranjit Singh, which stretched from Tibet to Afghanistan. Ranjit stripped many of the town's celebrated Muslim tombs of their ornaments, and sent them off to decorate the Sikh's Golden Temple in Amritsar. After the First Sikh War, in 1845, a British unit was stationed in Lahore: Henry Lawrence – one of three brothers, all of whom were to distinguish themselves in India, and leave a lasting mark on the Punjab in particular – was appointed the first British Resident. Four years later, after the final collapse of Sikh power in the Second Sikh War, Dilip Singh resigned his government to the British.

At about that time the sardonic traveller, Hugo James, came to Lahore; he noted that, under the Sikhs, Lahore was a centre of gaiety in which 'debauchery of every description, crime of every line and form, reigned with unblushing effrontery . . .' I'm proud to say that, apart from being the capital of the Punjab, it was the place in which, in 1940, the Muslim League made the first formal demand for a separate Muslim homeland which in 1947 came into being as Pakistan.

Lahore has always had a very special atmosphere – indeed, throughout its history travellers have described it as a city with a particular soul. Much of this derives from the Old City, which was once walled, with eight gates, and provided a resting place for travellers, traders and armies on their way from Delhi to Kabul, and back again. It may be dusty and polluted, but – quite apart from its remarkable buildings,

OVERLEAF *Lahore railway station.*

75

like the great Badshahi Mosque – it has always produced excellent musicians and first-rate cooking: my two great pleasures in life, together with shooting. Sadly, the Old City's character is being gradually destroyed by some horrendous modern architecture; and I do congratulate my friend Yusaf Salahuddin for pioneering attempts to conserve its buildings. His family used to live in two wonderful *havellis* (country houses); one of them has been destroyed and replaced with a dreadful cinema, but he has managed to preserve the other, and it is a fascinating place to visit. He is trying to interest the Government in preserving other *havellis* in the Old City, but I suspect that – as elsewhere in the Third World – conservation will be low on its list of priorities.

Since Partition Lahore has rapidly spread beyond the Old City and towards what was the British part of town. Luckily the new Lahore

Aitcheson College, Lahore, where I went to school.

78

has retained much of the character of the Old City. This is partly because the British created the Lawrence Gardens (now Baghi Jinnah), Aitcheson College, and a few other attractive buildings; and partly because General Jilani, the Governor of Lahore in the late 1970s, founded parks and planted a great many trees.

To the north-west of Lahore is the place that I particularly associate with my great hero, Sher Shah Suri: the great Rohtas Fort, on the Kaghan River. As his name suggests, Sher Shah Suri came from the Souri tribe of Pathans – a sister tribe to the Lodhis and to my own tribe, the Niazis. His grandfather had come down from the hills of Afghanistan, and had been given a grant of land by the Lodhis, who were then ruling India (this was shortly before Babur, the first Moghul Emperor, overthrew their dynasty). Sher Shah Suri's grandfather was given the land on the understanding that, in return, he would provide

A view from Lahore Fort.

79

soldiers to fight for the emperor when called upon to do so – a feudal system that was employed not only by the Lodhis, but by the Moghuls and the British as well. Sher Shah – whose real name was Farid Khan – acquired the name 'Sher' after killing a tiger with a sword. He inherited his father's modest estate, but he administered it so cleverly, and looked after his tenants so well, and was so good a soldier, that before long he had not only become a powerful local figure, but was able, in 1540, to defeat the great Babur's son, Humayun, and drive him into exile in Iran. Sher Shah Suri quickly took control of the Punjab, and built the Rohtas Fort as a defence against the Moghuls – Humayan later joined his two brothers in Kabul, and Sher Shah Suri feared that they would invade by way of the Khyber Pass and the

ABOVE *The enormous courtyard of the fort at Lahore, with the Badshahi Mosque in the background.*
RIGHT *Lahore Fort mosaic.*
OVERLEAF *The most revered Sufi of Punjab, Data Ganj Bakhsh.*

Peshawar Valley – and against the rebellious Gakhars, who lived in the Salt Range and remained loyal to the Moghuls. It was also the final nail in the coffin of the Kahers, who had lived off raiding caravans. The Gakhar chiefs, who had been on excellent terms with Babur and his family, had refused to attend a meeting with Sher Shah Suri, sending instead a lion cub and a bow and arrow – the implication of which was that they were the lions, and superior in arms. Sher Shah Suri was infuriated by this, and swore to take revenge. He inflicted terrible punishments on them, not least on their leader, Sarang Khan: not only did he bestow Sarang's daughter on his general, Khawas Khan, but he ordered him to be flayed alive and his body filled with straw. Not surprisingly, perhaps, the Gakhars did everything they could to hinder work on the Rohtas Fort: they unanimously agreed that no Gakhar would work for wages on its construction, and that

ABOVE *The Badshahi Mosque in Lahore.*

84

anyone who broke ranks would be killed. Nothing daunted, Sher Shah Suri entrusted Todar Mal, a Katri from Lahore, with its construction, and he started work on the Rohtas Fort in 1541. It was named after the Rohtasgarh Fort on the other side of the sub-continent, in Bengal, which Sher Shah Suri had captured in 1539, so prompting Humayun's flight from Delhi. (According to one story, Rohtasgarh was eventually captured after Sher Shah Suri had resorted to his own version of the Trojan Horse, sending his troops in under cover of palanquins or covered litters.) Rohtas is situated on the Grand Trunk Road, which Sher Shah Suri built from Delhi to the Peshawar Valley; he spent a fortune on building it, and it was only completed after his untimely death by Shahu Sultan. (My ancestor, Haibat Khan Niazi, spent a good deal of time at the Rohtas Fort, and helped in its construction.) Sher Shah Suri's death was suitably romantic. He was

ABOVE *Reciting the Holy Quran.*

besieging a Gakhar fort, inside which was a woman whose beauty was greatly admired. Sher Shah Suri was very worried that she might be killed in the siege, or even commit suicide, and he tried to persuade the defendants to surrender so that he could take her alive. While he was waiting for their response a shell fired from inside the fort, ricochetted off a wall and fell into a powder magazine – which promptly exploded, killing Sher Shah Suri, who was still only in his mid-thirties.

Sher Shah Suri held Humayun's throne for six years. He proved to be a great administrator and land reformer, though the Moghul Emperors often – and quite wrongly, in my view – get the credit for what he achieved. After his death the Pathans started feuding amongst themselves once again; and when Humayun eventually returned to Delhi from Kabul – proceeding, as expected, down the Peshawar Valley and the Grand Trunk Road – the then governor of Rohtas, Tartar Khan, made no effort to oppose him.

Built on a sandstone spur high above the river, Rohtas is a massive and imposing spectacle, covering 260 acres and with walls that are forty feet thick in places. It once boasted sixty-eight towers and twelve gateways, but it is now in a sad state: the sandstone on which it is built is not firm enough, with the result that huge cracks have appeared in the walls, and whole sections have collapsed. Once again, as with the palaces of Pakistan, there is no real policy of conservation or preservation. The government has acted to prevent the village of Rohtas from encroaching still further on the Fort; but unless something is done soon one of the most magnificent and historical forts in the country will disappear for good.

Less than a hundred miles to the west is Mianwali, where my father's tribe, the Niazis, settled in the thirteenth and fourteenth centuries, and where they have remained ever since, sandwiched between the Waziris on the North-West Frontier and the Punjabis on the west bank of the Indus. As I mentioned earlier the Niazis reached the peak of their power under Sher Shah Suri, when Haibat Khan Niazi was the Governor of Punjab. Sher Shah Suri would have completed the subjugation of the

Gakhar country up to the Indus had he not heard that the governor of Bengal was planning to rebel against him, so he had to leave the work to others – and in particular to Haibat Khan Niazi, the only person who had been able to keep the turbulent Gakhars in check. But Haibat Khan's problems were by no means restricted to the Gakhars. In 1543, when Sher Shah Suri was away campaigning in Ranthambor, a Baluchi chief named Fateh Khan captured Multan. Haibat Khan Niazi expelled him from the city, for which Sher Shah Suri rewarded him with the title of Azim Humayun and appointed him governor of Multan. Not long afterwards he had to deal with another revolt, this time led by a Jat robber chief with the same name of Jateh Khan: a fortress was established at Shergarh – named after Sher Shah Suri – where a force was maintained to keep an eye on rebellious Baluchis, Jats and Langahs.

A pilgrim at the Badshahi Mosque.
OVERLEAF *The fort at Rhotas.*

After Sher Shah Suri's death, the Niazis backed the wrong side in the civil war that followed, bringing to a close Niazi domination of the Punjab and any real political influence. Sher Shah Suri died in 1545, and his second son, Jalal Khan was proclaimed ruler under the title of Sultan Islam Shah. Kutab Khan, the commander of the Kumaon Hills, had strongly backed Islam Shah's brother: he fled to the Punjab, where he joined forces with Haibat Khan Niazi, Khawas Khan and other rebels. Islam Khan marched against the Punjab; Khawas Khan deserted the Niazis on the eve of battle; despite their stubborn resistance, the Niazis were routed at the Battle of Ambala. Many of those who escaped were drowned in the river, and the remnant were pursued as far as Rohtas. Khawaja Vais Sherwani was appointed governor of the Punjab: but Haibat Khan Niazi still had considerable influence within the Punjab, and a large following beyond the River Jhelum. Sherwani was driven back from Rohtas to Lahore; Islam Shah sent him reinforcements, and the Niazis were defeated once again. By a curious irony, they now allied themselves with Sher Shah Suri's old enemies, the Gakhars – a worrying development for Islam Shah, since Haibat Khan's position within Afghanistan had grown stronger. Islam Shah moved in with a formidable army, but despite two years' campaigning they were unable to defeat the Gakhars. However, relations between the Niazis and the Gakhars had become strained once more, and Haibat Khan decided to try to move off to Kashmir. A fierce battle was fought at Sambla, in which Bibi Rabia, Haibat Khan's wife, played a heroic part: but the Niazis were outnumbered and overwhelmed. Haibat Khan, his wife and his brother were all killed, and their heads were sent to Islam Shah.

At one time Islam Shah toyed with the idea of destroying Lahore, as a former stronghold of the Moghuls, and moving his capital to Mankot. I'm glad to say he never put this into effect. After his death in 1553, the Pathans once again started feuding amongst themselves. His uncle, Muhammed Adil Shah, seized the throne; but his dominions

The Indus widens as it enters the Plains near Mianwali.

were collapsing into anarchy, and in 1555 Humayun – whom Sher Shah Suri had earlier sent into exile – was able to restore Moghul rule once again.

Despite their political eclipse the Niazis continued to think of themselves as a ruling race, and were known for their strong physiques. I remember the Nawab of Kalabagh telling me how he was once watching the athletes in the Olympic Games in Melbourne, and was immediately reminded of a game of *kabadi* in Mianwali – *kabadi* being a game that is widely played in the rural areas of Sindh and the Punjab – in that all the young Niazi men – and especially those from Daud Khel – had physiques exactly like the Olympic athletes. A great uncle of mine called Khan Beg Khan was particularly well known for his physique and his physical strength. In the 1920s and 1930s he worked as a police superintendent in the Salt Range, near Mianwali. At one time, a leopard was causing havoc in a small village, making off with goats and other livestock, and the villagers asked my uncle for help. Khan Beg Khan couldn't begin to understand why the villagers were so frightened of the leopard: 'There are so many of you,' he said: 'how can you possibly be scared of a simple leopard?' One day, when he was on tour in the area, the villagers told him that the leopard had just killed a cow, and was nearby. My uncle took three policemen with him, and rode off to see what he could do. They spotted the leopard on a ridge and my uncle began to approach the leopard, a pistol in his hand. By now the leopard, well used to terrorising the villagers, was quite fearless: it began to growl and hiss, warning my uncle not to come any closer. All of a sudden the leopard charged; my uncle fired and missed, and the next minute the leopard was on him. Two of the policemen ran away. Luckily my uncle was wearing a thick police overcoat (it was winter-time) and he managed to ram his watch down the leopard's mouth as it tried to go for his jugular. The leopard held onto my uncle's scalp with one paw, and tore at his legs with its

ABOVE *The Awan tribesmen of Kalabagh.*
BELOW *A woman wearing a typical Burqa headdress.*

93

hindlegs, and they rolled over and over on the ground. All this time my uncle was shouting at the leopard 'If you are the son of a *sher* (lion), then I am the son of a Niazi.' Eventually the leopard got on top of my uncle – at which point my uncle's orderly stuck his bayonet into the leopard's back. Furious, the leopard whipped round and went straight for the orderly, who was killed within a matter of seconds. This gave my uncle an opportunity to pick up his gun and bayonet; when the leopard charged again he stuck the bayonet into him and finally killed him. But it was really his greatcoat – and his steel watch – that had saved his life. He was given the highest police award for bravery and was in hospital for six months; afterwards he admitted that he hadn't realised how strong a leopard was in relation to its size. Be that as it may, he was an amazingly strong man – he was known to drag down a bull by its horns. He only died about ten years ago, aged a hundred.

Like most Pathans, the Niazis have always enjoyed soldiering, and even now they make a disproportionately large contribution to the Pakistan army. At the time of the Sikh Wars, in the 1840s, the Niazis fought alongside the British – like most of the Muslims of Punjab and the North-West Frontier, they disliked and resented Sikh rule. They weren't too bothered by the British provided they didn't trouble them and left them well alone. They found British rule less oppressive than that of the Sikhs, but at the time of the Indian Mutiny in 1857 the Niazis on the east bank, unlike the Isakhel Niazis on the west bank, refused to join up to help quell the Mutiny, with the result that the British granted a good deal of land to the Isakhel Niazis, whereas in Mianwali the Niazis stayed poor. The Niazis also proved unco-operative in the 1920s, when their regiment, together with the Baluchi (composed basically of Waziris) and the Afridis from the North-West Frontier, refused to fight against the Turks just after the First World

The Nawab's Guest House at Kalabagh; view from the bridge with the Salt Range in the background.

War, on the grounds that they were fellow-Muslims, with the result that all three regiments were disbanded.

Life in Mianwali used to be very hard, with extremes of heat and cold; and until irrigation was introduced the area was pretty infertile, with desert all around. For many years the Gakhars – Sher Shah Suri's old enemies – were the overlords of Mianwali, and feudatories of the Moghuls. Jats from Sindh colonised the area in the seventeenth century, and they were followed in turn by Baluchis, who formed a kind of military caste over the Jats. Mianwali was incorporated into the Afghan Durrani kingdom in the eighteenth century, and was annexed by the British in 1849, after the Second Sikh War.

Not far from Mianwali, on the Indus, is the town of Kalabagh, where – as I said in my introduction – the river suddenly widens out and changes from a swiftly moving torrent to the broad, sluggish river we have become used to in Sindh and the Lower Punjab. Kalabagh is at the foot of the Salt Range: the salt is quarried on the surface and not mined as elsewhere in the Salt Range. The houses are built out of rock salt; they are built in tiers up against the side of a steep hill, the roofs of one tier forming the street for the tier above. All round Kalabagh is barren yellow desert, but just where the Indus widens there is a sudden burst of vegetation, an unexpected jungle in the middle of all this dryness. Dravidian survivors, not unlike those at Lake Manchnar, can be found living along the river near Kalabagh; they graze their buffalos on islands in the river, bringing the milk back to the shore on reed rafts.

Kalabagh has long been a crossing point of the Indus, first by ferry and then by bridge. The Nawab of Kalabagh's family used to levy the toll on the ferry: they were well advised to keep on good terms with the reigning power, whether Sikh or British, with the result that they were able to maintain their wealth and influence in the area. One of the Nawab's four sons went to school with me, and I still go shooting

The bridge at Kalabagh.
OVERLEAF *Kalabagh.*

with him in the Salt Range. The Nawab runs his estates very well, making the best possible use of modern technology, and he has also preserved his hunting reserve in the most admirable way. As I mentioned earlier, the Salt Range is teeming with game, but the Nawab – to his credit – very carefully regulates the amount of shooting he allows. He has the most wonderful guest house on the Indus, which was built between the wars. I only shoot partridge, but he has all sorts of game on his estate, like a mountain sheep called the hourial; and chenkara deer, which he has introduced to the area. One also finds black buck, which used to be found all over India but has been virtually hunted to extinction; and he is trying to introduce pheasants as well.

For me, one of the most dramatic incidents in our history occurred on the Indus between Kalabagh and Attock. Jalaluddin was a young Pathan prince who had inflicted a good deal of damage in Afghanistan on the invading Mongol army, with the result that a very much larger army was sent against him under Genghis Khan. Jalaluddin was forced to retreat back into India, and found himself surrounded by the Mongol army, with the river at his back. Like a cornered tiger, he charged into the middle of the Mongol army with his bodyguards, cut his way back to the river, recaptured his standard, and then – since there was nowhere else to go – leapt on his horse over a sixty-foot cliff into the Indus below. His horse's belly burst open when it hit the water, but Jalaluddin swam across the river to the other side. When Genghis Khan saw this, he was so impressed by the young man's bravery that he ordered his men not to fire, since so brave a man didn't deserve to die, and Jalaluddin made his way to India and safety.

Attock itself is dramatically situated on the heights above the Indus, which narrows down here, hurtling through a steep gorge little more than two hundred yards wide. The Kabul River joins the Indus just above Attock; opposite the town a whirlpool eddies between two jutting precipices of black slate known as Kamalia and Jalalia, after two Roshania heretics who were thrown from their summits during the reign of the emperor Akbar.

In the sixth century BC Scylax – the admiral despatched by the Persian emperor, Darius – swept through Attock on his way to the sea: he built his boats on the Kabul River, near Peshawar, and it took him two and a half years to make his way down the Indus and eventually back to Suez. Nearly two thousand years later, in 1581, the Moghul emperor Akbar arrived in Attock, and his huge army – including 500 elephants – was somehow ferried across the river. Akbar not only established a regular ferry service where the river narrows – not surprisingly, the ferry boats were frequently dashed against the rocks – but decided to build the great Fort at Attock to help protect his empire against his brother Hakim Mirza, the governor of Kabul. Attock Fort was completed in 1586: its high crenellated curtain walls are more than a mile in circumference. According to tradition, Akbar thought Attock impregnable, and so named it 'atak' or 'the obstacle'; on the opposite bank he founded Khairabad or the 'abode of safety', where the Sikhs – then expanding their empire – founded a second fort after Ranjit Singh had captured Attock Fort in 1812. He was held up by a raging Indus, on the right bank of which was a force of Yousafzai and Khattak Pathans. The Sikhs were unwilling to ford the river since the current was so strong; the Pathans tried to taunt them into attempting what would be a very dangerous crossing, given the turbulent state of the lion river. At last Ranjit Singh's general, Ahali Phoola Singh, could stand the Pathans' taunts no longer, and led the elite Sikh cavalry into the river. Although he lost a good many men and much of his equipment, he managed to cross to the other side, where a fierce battle began. The Afghan army watched from a distance, but did not come to the aid of the Pathans, who were eventually defeated, so enabling Ranjit Singh to march into the Peshawar Valley. Not surprisingly, Ahali Phoola Singh's daring crossing of the Indus resulted in his being widely admired for his courage and military brilliance.

OVERLEAF *The ruins of a Jain temple overlooking the village of Mari.*

Twenty years later, in 1832, Alexander Burnes crossed by the ferry on his way to Afghanistan, Persia and Bokhara; but it wasn't until 1883 that the British at last built a bridge at Attock. It hangs some hundred feet above the river, in case the breaking of a glacier, dam or a rock slide further up-river sends a bore or tidal wave rushing downstream – even so it has been nearly submerged more than once. Further evidence of British rule lies in the Victorian cemetery, and in the coats of arms of British regiments who fought on the North-West Frontier, which have been let into the rock on the right bank of the Indus, opposite the town.

Some sixteen miles to the north of Attock is the village of Hund. Once north of Kalabagh, the Indus is increasingly hemmed in by mountains, but at Hund the hills fall away and the river widens out. It was here that Alexander the Great is thought to have first crossed the Indus on a bridge of boats in 325 BC, and the Hund crossing was regularly used by armies invading India. Nothing now remains of the fort at Hund, but the local people are always coming across coins and other remains of those who passed through hundreds and even thousands of years ago.

Entrance to the fort at Attock.
OVERLEAF *The fort at Attock.*

PART 3

The North-West Frontier

Nowhere in Pakistan has a more romantic or exciting reputation than the North-West Frontier – the land of the Pathans, of the Khyber Pass, and of the Great Game that was fought out until well into this century between the British, the Russians, the Chinese and the Afghans. Yet although one tends to think only in terms of bare, rocky mountains, and isolated forts, and turbaned Afridi tribesmen settling ancient scores, the North-West Frontier Province – which was separated from the Punjab in 1901 – also includes, in the Kabul

Valley and the country round Peshawar, some of the most lush and fertile country in Pakistan. It is also a country through which, over the centuries, wave after wave of invaders have passed on their way through from the bleak uplands of Central Asia and Afghanistan to the plains of the Indus Valley and Central India – from the Persians and the Greeks of Alexander the Great to the Huns, the Scythians, the Mongols and the Turks.

Although there is a tradition that the Pathans are one of the lost tribes of Israel, most Pathans believe that they originated in Afghanistan – where, indeed, the majority of them still live, though there are some four million in Pakistan, the result of a movement of tribes down from the hills between the thirteenth and the sixteenth centuries. Pathans belong to various tribes, like the Niazis or the Lodhis, the members of which can trace a common ancestry through the male bloodline; each tribe is sub-divided into clans, sub-clans and patriarchal families. Tribal genealogies establish rights of succession and inheritance, and the right to speak in tribal councils and to use tribal lands. Disputes over property, women or whatever often lead to blood feuds between families: these may well be passed down from generation to generation unless the tribal councils intervene. Disputes are settled and punishments recommended by the *jirgah* or council of elders. Under the *jirgah* system – which must be one of the oldest forms of democracy in the world – the tribal elders decide matters by a show of hands, coming to their decisions by consensus rather than by a straightforward majority and providing their people with their only generally accepted form of law. Each tribe has at its head a *malik* or *khan* ('khan' meaning 'lion' or 'chief'), but here is no real system of chiefdom or hereditary

RIGHT *A tea house at Peshawar.*
PREVIOUS PAGE: LEFT *Almond blossom in the Baltistani orchards, approximately 8,000 feet above sea level.*
ABOVE *A familiar sight – a tanker truck bearing the portrait of a film star.*

rule: each individual considers himself to be, in effect, a chief and, given the Pathan spirit of independence, a tribal leader will be quickly abandoned once his followers lose confidence in him. It goes without saying that the Pathans – and especially those in the North-West Frontier – have little time or respect for any form of central authority, and their innate spirit of independence is reinforced by the individual's ownership of land. Conditions in the Hindu Kush and along the frontier have always been harsh; the tribes come together to fight the invader – whether Sikh, Moghul, British or, more recently, Russian – but once the external threat is removed feuding breaks out once again.

According to one theory, my mother's tribe – the Burkis – came to India from Afghanistan in the seventeenth century to avoid inter-tribal bloodshed. But another story has it that they were followers of Pir Roshan, and fought under him against the Moghuls. As we have seen, two of Pir Roshan's followers were thrown from precipices into the Indus at Attock; and once the Pir's rebellion had been crushed, the Moghuls decided to resettle some of the Burkis from their home in Karigoram – where the rest of the tribe still live – in forts outside the town of Jullander, which were known as 'bastis', with the result that they become known as the Basti Pathans.

When Ahmad Shah Abdali restored Afghan rule to the Punjab during the decline of Moghul power in the eighteenth century, he was supported by the Basti Pathans. On one occasion Ahmad Shah's son, Timur Shah, was returning to Lahore after defeating a Sikh army near Hoshiarpur, where he was based as Governor of the Punjab. Half his army had crossed the Sutlej – another tributary of the Indus – when he was attacked by a Sikh force led by Guru Barabagh Singh. Caught off guard, and with half his army on the other side of the river, Timur Shah was in a precarious position. He immediately sent word to the

TOP *The Qissa Khani Bazaar, Peshawar.*
BOTTOM *Armed tribesmen near the Khyber Pass.*

Basti Pathans for help: they came at once, and Guru Basabagh Singh was put to flight.

A few years later Ahmad Shah Abdali lay dying, and Timur Shah had to rush back to Kabul to claim his father's throne. This left the Punjab at the mercy of the Sikhs, who had by now grown into an awesome force, only kept at bay by the Pathans. No sooner had the Sikhs seized the Punjab than Guru Barabagh Singh sought revenge against the Basti Pathans. The three bastis within the town of Jullander were decimated, but those outside the town defended themselves with great vigour. But the Basti Pathans realised that they could not hold out for ever, as they were completely outnumbered and outgunned. They came to terms with the Sikhs, and so were able to survive.

The 'way of the Pathans' – the Pakhtunwali or Pashtunwali – is, in effect, the Pathan code of honour, the principles of which are rigidly adhered to. The most famous of these is *badal* or revenge. 'He is not a Pathan who does not give a blow for a pinch' the saying goes – an attitude that confirmed the Pathans' innately warlike tendencies, and made them so hard a people for the British or anyone else to rule, in that if a member of a tribe was killed by the British his life would have to be revenged. The second principle is *nanawatai*, or the right to seek asylum; and the third is *maelmastya*, according to which a stranger or even an enemy is entitled to hospitality. Each village will have its *hujra* or guest-house; it is essential to avoid disgracing a friend, relative or guest.

A well-known story shows just how seriously the Pathans take the need to be avenged. During the British Raj, a Pathan was sent off to the Andaman Islands for having committed what he felt to be a perfectly legitimate killing while avenging a long-standing family blood feud. He turned out to be a model prisoner, an honourable and gentle man who conducted himself with perfect dignity. After some years he was given more and more responsibility and freedom; officials on the island couldn't understand how such a decent man could have killed anyone, and he was allowed to go wherever he wanted and his sentence was reduced. But one day a senior British officer visited the

island, and was received with great ceremony. All of a sudden the
Pathan leapt upon him and stabbed him to death: somehow he held
him responsible for his unfair death sentence, and felt it his duty to
avenge himself. He was hanged, only a year before he was due to be
released.

Clad in their long shirts, waistcoats, trousers and turbans, a rifle
always in one hand, the Pathans of the Frontier province are instantly
recognisable – as are their wives in their baggy trousers, sporting nose
studs and silver necklaces. They must be among the most fiercely
independent and individualistic people on earth; and although the
British mounted endless expeditions against the tribes, destroying
their villages, crops and animals, and although they quite failed to
understand their ways or their ferocious code of honour, they greatly
admired them for their love of sport, their love of freedom, and their
utter disregard and defiance of all authority. Winston Churchill, who
spent some time as a soldier on the North-West Frontier, once wrote
that 'except at harvest time, when self-preservation enjoins a temporary truce, the tribes are always engaged in private or public war. Every
man is a warrior, a politician and a theologian'; and I described earlier
how, although the Moghuls and others relied on Pathan feudatories
or Jagirdars to provide soldiers with whom to rule India in exchange
for grants of land, the Pathan tendency to fight among themselves
prevented them from playing a dominant role in Indian political life,
at least after the death of Sher Shah Suri. Even so, for much of the
eighteenth century, after the collapse of Moghul power in the region,
much of what is now the North-West Frontier Province formed part
of the Pathan empire of the Afghan Durranis, based on Kabul. In 1818
Sikh rule replaced that of the Durranis in the North-West Frontier, up
to the Afghan border; while British concern about a possible French
– and later Russian – invasion of India via the North-West Frontier
made the entire area a focus of political influence and intrigue. Alexander Burnes's interest in opening up the Indus to navigation was, to
some extent, a cover for exploring the Frontier, while the Afghan
Wars of 1838 (in the course of which Burnes was murdered in Kabul,

and a British army massacred, with only one survivor) and 1877 reflected British anxieties about securing the North-West Frontier against the Russians. Quite how the 'Great Game' was played depended, to some extent, on whether the Liberals or the Conservatives were in power in Britain: Mr Gladstone preferred the 'Close Border' policy, according to which the frontier of British India would be, in effect, along the Indus, whereas the more expansionist Disraeli favoured the 'Forward Policy', which held the line on the Hindu Kush. In the event, the Forward Policy prevailed. The British had, in any event, annexed the North-West Frontier area after the Second Sikh War; in 1885, after the second Afghan War, a treaty of friendship was signed between the Amir in Kabul and Britain, and eight years later the Durand Line – which still defines the frontier – was finally agreed.

As fiercely independent as ever, the tribes themselves resented the

The famous Jamrud Fortress at the entrance to the Khyber Pass.

Afghans, the Sikhs, the British and, later, the Russians, who played them off against each other within the tribal areas to the east of the Afghan border – Khyber, Mohmand, North Waziristan and South Waziristan. Visitors to the area can hardly fail to be impressed by these lean, hawk-featured men – and not least in the bustling bazaars and streets of Peshawar, the capital of the North-West Frontier Province.

Since 1979, there has been a heavy influx of Afghan refugees, which has completely changed the life of the North-West Frontier Province in particular, and Pakistan in general. The Province became a major drug-producing area in the 1960s, when the demand for drugs in the West really took off; and to pay for arms to fight the Russians in Afghanistan, drugs – and heroin in particular – began to be grown and exported in much larger quantities than ever before. American aid comes with strings attached, but their efforts to control the drugs trade

A special briefing at the Khyber Pass.

have been largely unsuccessful; and the proliferation of drugs and drugs dealers has led to a proliferation of weapons, available in vast quantities at cheap rates.

There was an amusing story going round when I was in the Khyber Pass on my journey. It seems that – on American insistence – the Government was preparing to haul up a prominent Afridi drugs dealer. The dealer got wind of the Government's plans through his mafia, and immediately hired the services of 4000 Afghan *mujahadeen* – all of whose weapons had been supplied by the Americans. The Government realised that arresting the Afridi drugs dealer would involve a major army action against battle-hardened troops, and decided to leave well alone. I can't guarantee the authenticity of the story, though my

LEFT *The Swat Valley.*
ABOVE *A Swati girl.*
OVERLEAF *The remote Deosai Plains above Skardu,*
15,000 feet above sea level, which are covered in snow and
ice for most of the year.

informant was an officer of the Khyber Rifles, and would have taken part in the action against the dealer.

Situated in the middle of a fertile valley drained by the Kabul River, Peshawar was captured by Alexander the Great's general, Hephaestion, in 325 BC. For many years the valley was known by its ancient Hindu name of Gandhara; and the great age of Gandhara culture – which was to have an influence far beyond its frontiers – was the result of a unique combination of the Greek and the Buddhist. Buddhism became the official religion of Gandhara in the middle of the third century; but it was after its annexation by the Graeco-Bactrian king Eucratides that the flowing sculptures – redolent of both Greece and India – began to appear. It was a style that was to have great influence in China and Tibet, as was the local Mahayana school of Buddhism. Gandhara culture prospered until the collapse of the Kushan Empire in the middle of the third century AD, when the White Huns invaded, the Buddhist monks sought sanctuary, and the valley ceased – for the time being at least – to be a centre of trade and commerce.

Islam was brought to the Valley by the Turks: Sebuktigeen gained control of Peshawar in 988; his son was Mahmoud of Ghazni, who invaded India repeatedly between 1001 and 1027. It became part of the Moghul Empire under Akbar, who gave Peshawar its present name, meaning 'frontier town'. During the reign of Ranjit Singh, the town was governed – and considerably enlarged – by his famous Italian mercenary, Avitabile. In 1849, Peshawar was made the capital of a British District; it achieved fame as a garrison town, remembered by generations of British soldiers, and was named the capital of the North-West Province on its creation in 1901.

Peshawar has all the vigour and the colour of a frontier town, given over to smuggling as well as to legitimate forms of trade. The streets are awash with brightly painted trucks, many of them belonging to tribesmen from the hills; in addition to the large barracks area – the old British cantonment – there is a vast bazaar, whole sections of which are given over to particular types of metal work ('Bazaar of the Coppersmiths', Bazaar of the Goldsmiths' and so on). The city also contains the Buddha's begging pit, the holy pipal tree which is said to have given him shelter, and once had an enormous stupa, built by Kanishka, which served as a reminder of Gandhara's glorious past.

Just over ten miles to the west of Peshawar, at Jamrud, is one of the most famous landmarks in Pakistan – the Khyber Pass. Akbar Khan's forces defeated the Sikhs at Jamrud, and the great Sikh general, Hari Singh, was killed. The Khyber is the most northerly of all the passes leading from Afghanistan to Pakistan, and it twists and turns for thirty-three miles through the border hills until it reaches Dakka, on the Afghan side of the frontier. Its highest point, Landi Kotal, is only 3500 feet above sea level, and has been served once a week by a steam train from Peshawar since the 1920s. The Pass is wide enough for troops and cavalry to march through; and with the fertile Peshawar Valley at its eastern end, it's hardly surprising that it has always provided a much-favoured route for armies moving eastwards from the aridity of Central Asia to the lush promise of the Indian plains. Darius I, the emperor of Persia, came through the Khyber Pass; so too did Alexander the Great's generals, Hepaestion and Padiccas (though Alexander himself followed the Kabul River, then crossed the Kunar Valley into Bajaur and Swat), Babur, Humayun and Ahmed Shah Durrani. The Afridi Pathans proved incorrigibly troublesome. The Moghuls, who attached great importance to the Khyber, were as unable to control them as were, later, the Sikhs or the British. Nor did the Moghuls fare any better, for in 1692 a Moghul army was waylaid, 40,000 men killed and women, children, elephants and treasure taken into captivity. The British first advanced into the Khyber in 1839, when at the outset of the First Afghan War Captain Wade escorted to Kabul the British candidate for the Afghan throne, who temporarily replaced the more independent-minded Mohammed Dost. In the years leading up to the Second Afghan War, the Afghan government actively subsidised the Afridis in their feuds with the

OVERLEAF *The Indus near Skardu.*

British: the Amir, Sher Ali, summoned a *jirgah* of all Afridis and Shinwaris and distributed amongst them 5000 rifles with which to harass the British troops who were trying to keep open the Khyber Pass. In 1878 the British invaded Afghanistan via the Pass; when, a year later, the Treaty of Gandamak brought to an end the Second Afghan War, the British decided to leave control of the Pass to the tribes, with caravans being escorted by local levies – who later formed the basis for the well-known Khyber Rifles.

Further north from Peshawar is the remote and lovely valley of Swat. One enters Swat via the vertiginous hairpin bends of the high Malakand Pass; where the valley is at its widest is open, fertile country, a brightly coloured land of wild flowers and woods and crops which, sad to say, is suffering the familiar blight of deforestation and over-population. According to the Pathan poet Khushal Khan Khattak, Swat is 'meant to give kings gladness': the Buddhist monks who fled there in the fifth and sixth centuries A D to escape from the marauding

A goatherd and his flock.

126

White Huns considered the Valley a foretaste of Paradise, and it's not difficult to see what they meant. Like the Kabul Valley, Swat has strong associations with Buddhism: indeed, Buddhism was not replaced by Islam until the eleventh century – later than elsewhere in Pakistan. According to Buddhist tradition, the Buddha came to Swat in his last incarnation, preaching and performing miracles. Above the town of Jehanabad, a 1500-year-old Buddha is carved in the rock face, and the Butkara ruins outside the town of Saidu Sharif are on the site of an ancient Buddhist temple. More recently, Churchill saw action with the Malakand Field Forces against the rebel Yusafzais in 1897 (the tribesmen here, and as far north as Gilgit, are quite as quarrelsome and as independent-minded as those of the North-West Frontier). Until 1969, Swat was an autonomous princely state.

Perhaps the most famous – and remote – of British India's outposts in the nineteenth century was Gilgit, in the very far north of Pakistan. It is surrounded by some of the highest mountains in the world (Nanga Parbat, the eighth highest, is only thirty miles away), and nearby the jade-coloured Gilgit River flows into the dark grey Indus. Below Gilgit the Indus rushes through vast, perpendicular gorges into which the sunlight only reaches for an hour or two a day: its flow – and those of its tributaries, like the Gilgit or the Astor – is made more turbulent still by flooding and tidal bores, caused by glaciers and landslides blocking the river further upstream, especially if the summer monsoon coincides with the melting of the high glaciers. Gilgit itself is hot and dusty in summer, and cold and muddy in winter; the roads are frequently blocked by landslides or washed away by floods. And yet the Gilgit Valley itself, in the twenty miles before the river joins the Indus, is relatively sheltered – so much so that apricots, walnuts, grapes and melons are grown, as well as apples, mulberries, wheat,

Indus Valley village girls.
OVERLEAF *An aerial view of the Indus Valley, where the river enters Pakistan from Ladakh. The fields are terraced to retain moisture and reduce soil erosion.*

barley, maize, potatoes and turnips. Apricots provide a staple fare: they are eaten fresh in summer and dried in winter, while their kernels are either eaten like nuts, or converted into oil or flour. It has become altogether more accessible since the construction of the Karakoram Highway, which I saw being built in 1967, when I went to Gilgit and Hunza on a school trek.

The inhabitants of Gilgit are lighter-skinned than most of their compatriots – giving rise, predictably enough, to suggestions that they may be descended from Alexander the Great's soldiers (a ruined stable in Gilgit Town is said – improbably – to have been built by the Greeks). Maybe the fact that they make and drink their own wine is further evidence of their Mediterranean origin? In Gilgit itself they tend to live in square, pale-coloured houses, the roofs of which are covered with snow in winter and, in summer, with hay and chillies laid out to dry. Like other tribes in their part of Pakistan, they had – until recently – a wild and ferocious past; they remain keen huntsmen, whether with hawk or gun, as well as the dashing and dangerous originators of polo. Every now and then the town is given over to polo tournaments: the matches are preceded by tent-pegging, and accompanied on pipes and drums.

For many years the inhabitants of Gilgit were ruled by the Maharajah of Kashmir, whom they greatly resented. In 1877 the British established the famous Gilgit Agency, to protect their interests against the Rajah and, more importantly – for Gilgit was considered to have a key part to play in the Great Game – to keep an eye out for Russian spies and soldiers. The Agency was abolished in 1881, but re-established eight years later when Algernon Durand – who gave his name to the frontier that separates Afghanistan and Pakistan – was appointed Agent, responsible for Gilgit, Baltistan and all points north and east. The Agents recruited a small military-cum-police force, the Gilgit Scouts, who wore Black Watch tartans and boasted their own pipe

*The Indus Valley: Children returning from school through
the sand dunes that surround Skardu.*

band; much later, at the time of Partition, they were to play a heroic role in keeping Baltistan on the Pakistani side of the border. As the last town before the Chinese border, Gilgit with its busy bazaar remains a centre of trade: the road up the Indus and then on to the Chinese border was completed in 1968.

And so we come to our final point of call on our long journey up the Indus – Skardu, the capital of Baltistan, high up in the mountains where the Himalayas and the Karakoram meet. Here the Indus Valley is 7500 feet above sea level; a tributary, the Shigar, runs down from the Karakorams to join it near Skardu, while another, the Shyok, has its origins in the Ladakh Mountains. The valley in which Skardu is situated is twenty miles long and eight miles wide, with narrow gorges at either end through which the Indus runs. The valley floor is carpeted in fine sand, and the Indus weaves its way between sand dunes. It is a bleak, windswept land of rock and sand and snow, of pale white light and a biting dry wind. The rivers are fed from the glaciers, and carry with them a flotilla of small icebergs. This is a region of earthquakes and storms, in which cataclysms occur when the summer melt loosens the ice, and mud and boulders pour down into the valley. Villages are perched up the side of the valley, to avoid torrents and landslides; the mountains around are the haunt of the fabulous snow leopard, the *ram chukor* (a game bird from the partridge family, found near the snow line), the rare Monal pheasant, reputed to be the most colourful in the world, the Marco Polo sheep and the golden sheep.

The people of Baltistan look very much like Tibetans, but are Muslim rather than Buddhist. Surprisingly, perhaps, the valley is far more green and fertile than its climatic rigours might suggest. Cultivation is an arduous business, but in the Shigar Valley the Baltistanis grow wheat, maize, barley, melons, nuts, melons and nectarines – all of which are floated down river to the market in Skardu on rafts consisting of a wooden frame supported on inflated goatskins (which are reinflated *en route* by blowing down the legs).

Fruit trees in blossom in the Shikar Valley.

Easily the most impressive spectacle in Skardu itself is an enormous, Gibraltar-shaped rock, on the top of which perches the Askandria Fort. It was captured by Gulab Singh in the first half of the nineteenth century, after which Baltistan became a province of Kashmir. In 1947 the Baltistanis finally revolted against the Maharajah of Kashmir, who was anxious that Kashmir should, after Partition, become part of India rather than Pakistan: a force from Gilgit captured the Askandria Fort, with the result that Skardu and Baltistan – unlike neighbouring Ladakh, to the east – remained on the Pakistani side of the cease fire line.

Even today, the road from Gilgit to Skardu is fit only for jeeps, and the 120-mile journey takes fourteen hours: the flight from Islamabad – which must be one of the most dramatic in the world, following the Indus Valley, with the snow-capped mountains towering up on either side – takes only an hour, but is so dangerous that only the most skilful pilots are allowed to undertake it, and it is often cancelled because of

ABOVE *Bread-making in the village of Shigar.*
RIGHT *Baltistani shepherd.*

the weather. (Recently a Fokker disappeared without trace.) When I went there with Mike Goldwater we had hoped to be able to hire helicopters from which to photograph the dramatic mountain scenery. Unfortunately, we were unable to do so, since there is still a war going on with India. It was being fought, in this case, on the Siachen Glacier – at 20,000 feet, the highest war being fought anywhere on earth. This undeclared war – essentially a border dispute over uninhabited land – has been rumbling on for the past six or seven years. Most of the casualties on both sides result from the weather rather than exchanges of fire. We got to know a good many of the soldiers there – including some helicopter pilots, who took us up and let us take our photographs – and as I talked to them I felt in them a kind of patriotism I hadn't been aware of since I was about thirteen years old, at the time of the Indo-Pakistan War of 1965. I'll never forget the waves of patriotism that swept through us then. In those days Zaman Park, our home in Lahore, had only eight houses in the Park, and all of them belonged to relatives of mine. I remember we held a council of war in my uncle's house, and although I was so young I insisted on being allowed to go along. Since Lahore is only thirteen miles from the border, we decided that we must protect ourselves against a possible parachute landing by the Indians, and that every gun in our possession should be at the ready. I was considered – much to my shame and mortification – too young to do guard duty; I felt desperately envious of my eighteen-year-old cousin Majid, who was allowed to take his turn. One night I sneaked out of our house, determined to do my bit, and was ambushed by Majid and the other guards.

I remember, too, that one of my uncles – a very warlike individual – challenged two men who were walking down the street in the middle of the night. He asked them who they were, quite misunderstood their reply, and immediately fired at them. Luckily he was a rotten shot and missed them both . . .

All that was twenty-five years ago; but in the years since, my love and fascination for Pakistan and its people has grown ever greater. I make no pretence to be a scholar, or to have written a thorough and

exhaustive account of the Indus and its tributaries, or the towns along its length: my book is, inevitably, both selective and subjective, a very personal evocation of, and reaction to, the country which inspired such feelings in me as a would-be schoolboy soldier in Lahore and on the bleak glaciers of the Karakoram, as well as on the cricket field.

And so our Indus Journey comes to a close, in a very different world from that in which we started out. The 'lion river' is the backbone of Pakistan, and along its length can be found a rich and astonishing variety of scenery, climate, people, cultures, animals and plants. If my book helps to persuade the Pakistani Government to do all it can to preserve so rich and unique a heritage – and others to come and see it for themselves – I shall feel I have not written it in vain.

The Rakaposhi peak, 26,000 feet above sea level.
OVERLEAF *The Indus less than 50 miles from the border with China.*

Acknowledgements

The author would like to thank the Pakistan Ministry of Tourism, Pakistan International Airline, Mr Hamid Akhund, Azam Khan of Kalabagh, General Rana of the Frontier Force, Colonel Awan at Attock Fort, and Ashiq Qureshi.

The publishers would like to thank Bryn Campbell, Humayun Gauhar, Maxine Gremson, Nigel Horne, Jeremy Lewis, Pervez A. Khan, Shahid Qadir and all at Network Photographers.

All photographs © Mike Goldwater except page 37, lower picture, © Abdul Hamid Akhund and pages 120–21, page 139, © Pervez A. Khan.